Chore Sports

by Lilly Cho
illustrated by Carolyn Croll

Practice Decodable 37

I0806514

McGraw Hill Education

Bothell, WA • Chicago, IL • Columbus, OH • New York, NY

MHEonline.com

Send all inquiries to:
McGraw-Hill Education
8787 Orion Place
Columbus, OH 43240

ISBN: 978-0-02-137236-2
MHID: 0-02-137236-5

Printed in China.

8 9 10 11 12 DSS 27 26 25 24 23

I did chores and had fun.

I sorted socks as a sport.

I sorted fast!

I picked corn as a sport.
I picked corn fast!

I fixed lunch as a sport.

Can I get forks out fast? I can!

I did more for Mom.
I helped at the store.

I finished the chores.

I had fun!